I Like Biographies!

Read About
Martin Luther King, Jr.

Stephen Feinstein

Enslow Publishers, Inc.

40 Industrial Road   PO Box 38
Box 398   Aldershot
Berkeley Heights, NJ 07922   Hants GU12 6BP
USA   UK

http://www.enslow.com

Words to Know

civil rights—The rights given to all the people of a country.

equality—Having the same rights and laws for everyone.

minister—A teacher of religion.

mob—A big crowd of people.

preach—To speak about religion.

violence—Acts that hurt or destroy people or things.

Library of Congress Cataloging-in-Publication Data

Feinstein, Stephen.
  Read about Martin Luther King, Jr. / Stephen Feinstein.
    v. cm. — (I like biographies!)
  Includes bibliographical references and index.
  Contents: A childhood in the south— Martin becomes a minister—Fighting for civil rights — "I have a dream"— Timeline.
  ISBN 0-7660-2300-1
  1. King, Martin Luther, Jr., 1929–1968—Juvenile literature.
2. African Americans—Biography—Juvenile literature. 3. King, Martin Luther, Jr., 1929–1968—United States—Biography— Juvenile literature. 4. Baptists—United States—Clergy— Biography—Juvenile literature. 5. African Americans—Civil rights—History—20th century—Juvenile literature. [1. King, Martin Luther, Jr., 1929-1968. 2. Civil rights workers. 3. Clergy. 4. Civil rights movements—History. 5. African Americans—Biography.] I. Title. II. Series.
E185.97.K5F45 2004
323'.092—dc22
                              2003020010

[3]

Printed in the United States of America

10 9 8 7 6 5 4 3 2 1

To Our Readers: We have done our best to make sure all Internet Addresses in this book were active and appropriate when we went to press. However, the author and the publisher have no control over and assume no liability for the material available on those Internet sites or on links to other Web sites. Any comments or suggestions can be sent by e-mail to comments@enslow.com or to the address on the back cover.

Illustration Credits: AP/Wide World, pp. 1, 3, 13, 17, 19, 21; © Marjorie Collins/Corbis, p. 5; Library of Congress, pp. 9, 11; National Park Service, p. 7; © Flip Schulke/Corbis, p. 15.

Cover Illustration: AP/Wide World.

Contents

Martin Luther King, Jr., was born on January 15, 1929, in Atlanta, Georgia. When he was little, he liked to play ball with his friends.

Martin's best friends were white. But Martin was black. Martin could not sit next to his friends at the movies or on the bus. That was the law in the South.

Martin had to go to a school just for black children, like these students.

4

Martin went to church every Sunday. His father was the minister. Martin loved to hear his father preach. His father's words filled people with joy. The words made people sad or angry. They also made people think.

This is the church where Martin's father was the minister. Martin liked to go to church and hear the words from the Bible.

Martin wanted to use words to make the world a better place. Black people did not have the same rights as whites. That was wrong. Martin wanted to help black people fight for the same rights as white people.

"Colored" is an old word for black. This sign means that black people had to drink out of this fountain.

Martin decided to become a minister like his father. At college, he learned about Gandhi, a man in India. Gandhi showed people how to change unfair laws without violence. Martin thought this was the best way for black Americans to gain their rights.

After Martin became a minister, he went back to college. When he finished, he was called "Dr. King."

This is Gandhi, a man of peace. His actions gave Martin many ideas.

Chapter 3

Fighting for Civil Rights

In December 1955, in Montgomery, Alabama, a black woman named Rosa Parks refused to give up her seat on the bus to a white man. The police arrested her. Dr. King asked black people to stop riding the buses. The bus company lost money. Then the law was changed. Black people could sit anywhere on the bus.

When Rosa Parks was arrested, it made people angry. They wanted to change the law.

13

Dr. King gave speeches all over the South. He said that all people were equal under the law. Dr. King led many marches for civil rights. Civil rights are the rights given to all of the people in a country.

In 1953, Martin married Coretta Scott. Here she is with their children, Dexter, Bernice, Martin Luther King III, and Yolanda.

Even though the marchers were peaceful, they were often beaten by angry white mobs and arrested by police. Many people thought this was not fair. The laws were changed. Black people could sit, eat, and go to school where they wanted. And now they could vote.

Martin Luther King led many people to march for civil rights.

In 1963, there was a huge civil rights march in Washington, D.C. Dr. King told the crowd, "I have a dream that one day, little black boys and black girls will be able to join hands with little white boys and white girls and walk together as sisters and brothers."

Thousands of people came to hear Dr. King and other speakers.

Many people shared Dr. King's dream. But not everybody. On April 4, 1968, Dr. King was shot and killed in Memphis, Tennessee.

People all over the world were sad. We will remember Martin Luther King, Jr., for his bravery and good ideas.

Dr. King's hard work helped black people gain equal civil rights.

21

Timeline

1929—Martin Luther King, Jr., is born on January 15.

1947—Martin becomes a minister.

1953—Martin marries Coretta Scott on June 18.

1954—Dr. King begins preaching in Montgomery, Alabama.

1963—Dr. King leads civil rights march in Washington, D.C., on August 28.

1968—Dr. King is killed on April 4.

Learn More

Books

Frost, Helen. *Martin Luther King, Jr. Day.* Mankato, Minn.: Pebble Books, 2000.

Jackson, Garnet. *Martin Luther King, Jr.: A Man of Peace.* New York: Scholastic, 2001.

Rappaport, Doreen. *Martin's Big Words: The Life of Dr. Martin Luther King, Jr.* New York: Hyperion Books for Children, 2001.

Internet Addresses

Martin Luther King, Jr. Day on the Net
<http://www.holidays.net/mlk>

Martin Luther King, Jr.—Sites for Students
<http://www.thematzats.com/mlk>

Index